BORN IN THE 40s

BORN IN THE 40s

ARCTURUS

ARCTURUS

This edition published in 2014 by
Arcturus Publishing Limited
26/27 Bickels Yard, 151–153 Bermondsey Street,
London SE1 3HA

Copyright © 2013 Arcturus Publishing Limited

ISBN: 978-1-84858-884-7
AD004026UK

Printed in China

Contents

All photographs from **Getty Images** apart from those below:
Corbis (14, 54, 56, 78, 84); **Topfoto** (39, 53, 60, 63, 76, 98-99, 101, 144)

Introduction

• •

The Forties was a decade that drew a line down the middle of the 20th century, a watershed that saw radical changes in the British way of life. Indeed, it was a decade that was itself divided into two distinct halves: the war years and the post-war years. This book portrays the two sides of the Forties in vivid pictures and words that rekindle memories of those formative years.

It began with Britain already at war, being repelled by German forces in mainland Europe and living in constant fear of invasion. Families were split up, children separated from their mothers and fathers marched away to fight. Soon came the nightly dread of the Blitz, the blackouts and bomb shelters becoming familiar features of everyday life. Food was rationed, crime figures rose, mothers were widowed, children orphaned, whole neighbourhoods destroyed. But through it all the people dug in. They produced their own food, their own clothes, their own entertainment. The hardship gave rise to resilience and resourcefulness, to co-operation and community spirit and an acceptance of austerity for the sake of the collective good.

Then came the peace – and although the hard economic conditions continued throughout the decade, there emerged a growing sense of freedom and entitlement, of adventure and possibility. Women's rights took a significant step forward, the demands of women to play an equal part in society and the workplace proving irresistible in the light of the way they had taken on the work of men during the war. In 1948 Cambridge University awarded degrees to women for the first time ever!

That same year saw the founding of the National Health Service and the nationalization of the railways – the former a major breakthrough for the health of the nation as a whole, the latter an act of debatable effectiveness, though probably necessary as Britain emerged from the war with a rather run-down rail service, now facing growing competition from road transport. There was a growing desire for travel and discovery. The war had both taken people to new frontiers in foreign lands and brought in foreigners in unprecedented numbers, all joining the Allied war effort. As a result, the people's horizons had been broadened and, while overseas holidays were still the preserve of the privileged few, it wouldn't be long before the trains to seaside resorts were being diverted to the Channel ports and beyond. Like a seed that had lain dormant throughout a long, harsh winter, technologies and entertainments that had been stifled by the war now burst into life. Television, the motor car and domestic appliances all began to become available to a much wider market. Football and cricket, the national sports of winter and summer, were followed in large numbers and in 1948 the Olympic Games came to London. Britain was emerging back into the light. Fashions were reflecting this new sense of self-expression and merriment and the country, made tougher and more determined by war, was ready to grasp the future with both hands and make sure those dark days would never have to be endured again.

Wartime

The Second World War was the ever-present backdrop for children growing up in the first half of the Forties. Air raids, blackouts, rationing and absent fathers were all facts of life. Many children barely met their fathers before they were old enough to start school because they were off fighting for long periods in other parts of the world. Many others never met their fathers at all. Yet despite the bombings, the lack of luxuries and the loss, the war years are remembered by many who grew up then as a time of great excitement and adventure.

The Battle of Britain brought terrifying air raids, nights huddled in underground shelters, vast destruction and the constant fear of disaster, yet for the children who lived through it, it brought the thrilling spectacle of squadrons of planes flying high overhead and death-defying dogfights between Spitfires and Messerschmitts, flying incredibly low over the rooftops. Evacuation brought the opportunity for city children to experience a whole new way of life, often in beautiful country settings; and the regular reports coming in from the front meant stories of valour and heroism, which children emulated in their own imaginative games.

Left *A crocodile of children, all wearing identity tags and carrying their gas masks in innocent-looking cardboard boxes, make their way along London's sunlit streets to one of the mainline stations, to be evacuated to the relative safety of the countryside as the threat of German bombs looms large.*

Right *The smiles on the faces of these nine children beaming out of a train window belie the emotional trauma that evacuation brought with it. Though it was regarded as a great adventure for many of the children involved, for others the wrench away from home and parents was very unsettling.*

Leaving home

Two days before war was declared, Operation Pied Piper got under way. Its aim: to remove women and children from the cities that were expected to be targeted by German bombers. Over a period of four days, around three million people were relocated, mostly children. Though some mothers went along, mostly it was teachers who oversaw the allocation of evacuees to their new homes and in many cases they arrived off the trains to find chaos. Children were lined up in village halls while volunteer guardians chose which ones they wanted to take in. The words 'I'll take that one' became a familiar wartime catchphrase.

Not everyone went along with the idea of sending their children away at first, but in the summer of 1940 the growing threat of attack on Britain's coastal towns, coupled with the start of the Blitz, prompted a second wave of evacuations, which continued until 1944. In total, around 3.5 million people were relocated during the war, undoubtedly saving many lives, and for some even improving them.

The gas mask became part of every child's uniform during the war and everybody had to learn how to get the clumsy items out of their boxes and fit them properly. The big eye holes and mute noses gave children the look of cartoon aliens, an endearing yet terrifying image.

War meant a whole new routine. Many young children spent their days together in newly formed crèches while their mothers went out to work. This group in Northampton saying grace before dinner are the children of women who took up jobs in the local factories to help the war effort.

Working women

A lasting legacy of the war was to change attitudes towards women and work. Until then most married women were expected to be housewives and few jobs were deemed suitable for women at all. Nurse, shop assistant or domestic servant was about the scope of it. But with so many men called up to fight and no longer able to carry out their regular jobs, it became necessary to fill the huge gaps in the workforce with women. Single women between the ages of 20 and 30 were called up to join the workforce and they were soon joined by married women, 80 per cent of whom showed their determination to enlist in the war effort. Milkmen, postmen, bus conductors and station guards were all replaced by women, but it didn't end there. Women proved themselves more than capable of doing the heavy work their menfolk had been doing in factories, shipyards and even the Armed Forces, and the Women's Land Army played a crucial role in ensuring that there was enough food being produced from Britain's farms.

Keep calm and carry on! These girls manage to continue their skipping game unhindered by the gas masks they're wearing. Gas masks were an ever-present feature of wartime and were stashed away in attics when fighting ended, often coming to light decades later, discovered by inquisitive grandchildren.

There was no shortage of adventure for children and with far greater dangers raining down from the skies every night, they were allowed to pursue some rather hair-raising games. These boys are grabbing a ride on the back of a London carriage, running the risk of some severe knee grazing.

Three sisters from London forget the fact that they've had to spend Christmas away from home as they get their hands on the first lambs of the year at the farm they've been evacuated to in Sussex. Such experiences created fond memories for children and left them reluctant to return to the city.

A teacher administers medicine to the evacuated children in his care. Teachers became the principal supervisors during the evacuation operation, taking the place of parents in helping children to settle in their new homes and trying to ensure the safeguarding of health and happiness during those difficult times.

The Land Girls

A working party from the Women's Land Army takes a break to watch a squadron of fighter planes return home from a sortie over France. One of the more romantic images of the war is that of the army of women who went to work on the land, their hair tied back with a headscarf, sleeves rolled up, hoe in hand, making the arduous toil of tilling the soil look like the pinnacle of femininity. And in many ways it was. Around 80,000 recruits joined the Women's Land Army during the war and earned the respect and adoration of the nation by playing a vital role in keeping the people fed.

War brought a two-fold pressure on farmers: firstly, it took away most of the men who had made up the agricultural workforce and, secondly, it increased the demand for domestic food production since the import of goods across hostile seas was hit hard. Land Girls were supposed to work a maximum of 50 hours a week (48 in winter), for which they were paid 28 shillings plus food and lodging.

Left *A pretty girl bearing a tray of teas – the ultimate tonic for the troops – offers liquid refreshment to two Canadian soldiers as they prepare to set sail for France. The uniforms and accents of overseas troops became common sights and sounds as Britain was joined in the war by allies from the Commonwealth.*

Right *A British sergeant hugs his wife and son on his return from the war in Burma in 1945. For many children born during the war, moments like these were the first time they had met their father and the thrill of his safe return was tempered by the adjustment to having a new man about the house.*

PEACE AT LAST *Jubilant crowds gather in London's Piccadilly to celebrate Victory in Europe on 8 May 1945. A few months later Japan surrendered and the war was finally over; now for the peace. The conflict had dominated the first half of the decade but now the Forties was entering its second phase.*

The Forties was a decade spent surviving and rebuilding and children were expected to play their part. Discipline was strict, luxuries few, yet children enjoyed a sense of freedom and adventure that would seem liberal by today's standards.

Little Angels

The scarcity of cars meant the street was a safe place to play and for many children it was the principal playground. Television was still extremely rare so the main entertainments were those you made for yourself, usually outdoors, often around the bombsites or the empty buildings left after the war. For mothers, many of whom had been left husbandless after the war, happiness meant knowing your children were out from under your feet and as long as they came home in time for tea, no questions were asked. If they were good they might get a slice of pie or cake, rations permitting, but they would be expected to clear up after meals and to help with other chores around the home. But not all children in the Forties were little angels – tight boundaries just meant more opportunities for a spot of mischief.

Who's who?

The last year of the war saw a rise in the number of births to the highest level in 21 years. Many children born in the first half of the Forties came into the world fatherless and the difficulty of raising a child single-handed forced a lot of mothers to give their newborn children up for adoption – a heart-rending experience that was generally regarded as preferable to the disgrace of being branded a single mother.

Even for the lucky ones where the family unit was intact, childbirth in the Forties was no picnic. The labour itself was a very prescriptive process. Mothers were not encouraged to plan their own birthing experience complete with candles and music; instead they followed doctor's orders and battled through the pain with little more than a few breathing exercises to help them. Fathers were certainly not expected to attend the birth and once the babies were born they were whisked away to the nursery where they would be supervised by the nursing staff and only reunited with their mothers at feeding time.

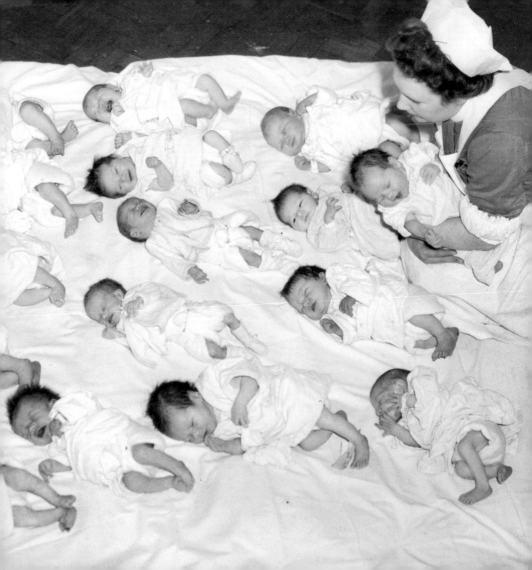

Above *A baby wearing a typical towelling nappy shares a joke with the family dog. Children and animals got along in the Forties as well as they have done in any other decade and a dog with a hat on is funny in any era.*

Right *Children at an orphanage in Berkshire are given a ride by the gardener in his wheelbarrow, much to their delight. Though the war brought a sharp rise in orphaned children, orphanages began to close down in the Forties as fostering and adoption became more popular.*

Romance blossoms on a street corner. With no traffic to worry about except the occasional bicycle, parents were happy to let their children play in the street. This was the place where friendships were formed, adventures began and lasting memories were made.

Two children from Elephant and Castle in south London share the ultimate luxury of a piece of cake – home made, of course. Though the ingredients were rationed, mothers knew how to make the most of them and the look on these children's faces suggests the results were rather good.

Almost as if he hasn't noticed that his companion is a chimpanzee,
a young boy contemplates his picture book with intense concentration.
Sunshine, grass and a good book were just about all a small boy
needed in those days, though the chimp looks eager to turn the page.

Is the cup half empty or half full? These twin sisters appear to take differing
views of their day out for a picnic in the Essex countryside. Generally
speaking, a picnic was an eagerly anticipated highlight, especially for city
children who rarely got the chance to enjoy the great outdoors.

Left *A young waitress concentrates very hard as she negotiates the doorstep with her tray of drinks. From an early age, children were expected to do their bit around the home, helping to tidy, clean and cook, and developed useful domestic skills as a matter of course.*

Right *A boy tries not to flinch as his mother attacks his locks with a razor. Grooming was held in very high regard and children were expected to look trim and smart – even if they didn't act that way. All the boys had short hair like their fathers and usually it was mum who kept it that way.*

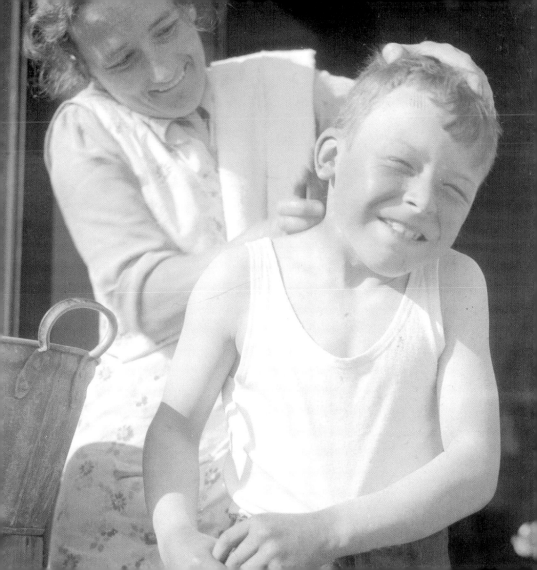

Sweet dreams

Sweets were rationed from 1942 throughout the Forties, right up until 1953 in fact, a situation that only added to their mystique and allure. Every child over the age of five was given an allowance of up to 7 oz of sweets per week, roughly the equivalent of one sweet per day. However, it was common practice for adults to donate their sweet ration coupons so that children could have more. The traditional confectioner's shop was an Aladdin's cave of big glass jars containing such wonders as aniseed balls, sarsaparilla tablets, pear drops, barley sugars, butterscotch, toffees and liquorice. Sweets were measured out on the scales and tipped into paper bags. Most of the time, though, a child's experience of the sweet shop was from the outside, gazing longingly through the window at all those colourful creations and dreaming of the day when they could go in and buy their rations. With sweets in short supply, it was a good time for teeth and the decade saw a greater focus on dental care, culminating in the introduction of free dentistry for children on the National Health.

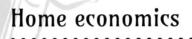

Home economics

Mastering the art of turning a limited food supply into a tasty and exciting diet became paramount during the Forties and nobody was too young to learn. Home economists from the Ministry of Food would tour the country demonstrating how to make the most of the food available, devising new recipes and promoting the more plentiful ingredients such as carrots and potatoes. As a result of rationing, the Forties diet became very healthy and very democratic. Mothers were told they were fighting on the 'Kitchen Front' and everyone rose to the challenge, recruiting their children to the cause as soon as they were old enough to wield a wooden spoon.

But when you had the chance to get your hands on a bit of 'luxury' food, you would jump at it. In 1943 a single banana was raffled for £5, the equivalent of a good week's wage! And people still wanted to fill up on cake. All sorts of new recipes were devised for eggless fruitcakes and sugarless sponges and home baking became one of the great triumphs on the Kitchen Front.

Mum's the word

A baby sleeps soundly on a London street, blissfully unaware that his welfare is in the hands of two little girls, only a few years older than he is. Not that he would have been particularly concerned because it was not at all uncommon for mothers to leave their babies unattended while they popped into the shops, or for young girls to play mother with real babies. Though the Forties did see the invention of some classic toys and games, including the Slinky and Scrabble, children were encouraged to go and play outdoors as much as possible. While young boys spent their play time fighting their own imaginary wars or emulating their sporting heroes, for girls one of the favourite pastimes was mimicking mum, which generally meant standing around chatting with your girlfriends while swinging your handbag or rocking baby in the pram.

The top five most popular names for boys born at this time were John, David, Michael, Peter and Robert, while for girls it was Margaret, Patricia, Christine, Mary and Jean.

ROAD TO NOWHERE *A group of boys from the Gorbals area of Glasgow strolls around the empty streets looking for an escape. Conditions in the Gorbals were vividly summed up in a 1948* Picture Post *article, which described it as Britain's most abandoned slum, with people living eight to a room and 30 to a single lavatory.*

WHEEEE!

Fight! Fight! Fight!

Two boys settle their differences in the time-honoured way. There are several points to note in this picture: 1, boys in the Forties did not wear long trousers, they wore shorts and thick woolly socks; 2, boys did not grow their hair long, they had it cropped short back and sides, with a modicum of growth on top; 3, the smaller kid appears to be giving the bigger kid a bit of a beating; 4, the group of boys who have gathered to watch appear to be enjoying it immensely, although one or two look rather relieved that it's not them in the fray.

Playground fights were not uncommon in the Forties as boys used the school environment to work off their frustration with one another or simply to spark a bit of excitement. As soon as the word went up that two boys were about to go at it, a crowd would quickly gather around them, leaving the protagonists with no opportunity to negotiate a peaceful settlement. The fights were often half-hearted affairs and when they were over the boys would mysteriously become the best of friends.

Two girls and a boy play skipping on an English street. The skipping rope was a key component of a girl's playthings, and every girl would know the rhymes and chants that accompanied their skipping games. For boys, all that was required was to hold one end.

A Boy Scout shines shoes for a shilling a time as part of Bob-a-job Week, a scheme introduced after the war to encourage young people to help their local community. Other typical jobs included gardening, cleaning and carrying things for old people. Money raised went towards camping trips and equipment.

Outlaws

• •

A gang of boys play with toy bows and arrows in a graveyard in Wapping. In densely populated areas like east London, the local graveyard was one of the few green spaces where children could play hide and seek amid the cover of trees and bushes, not to mention the gravestones. These boys look like they're preparing to play at being Robin Hood and his merry men, but the inspiration behind their weapon of choice could just as easily have been the American Indians, who were galloping across Britain's cinema screens with increasing regularity. The Forties saw the resurgence of the cowboy 'Western', spearheaded by actors like Roy Rogers and John Wayne, and the regular Saturday morning trip to the pictures provided all the inspiration children needed to spend the following week emulating the exploits of their screen idols.

Boys could get lost for hours playing Cowboys and Indians or Robin Hood and the only disputes came when someone got shot.

'You're dead.'

'No, I'm not.'

'You are, I shot you.'

'No, you only wounded me.'

The Forties saw major reforms to the education system, brought about by the 1944 Education Act. The most significant change in the Act was to make education free for all children up to the age of 15, thereby providing an equal opportunity for children across the board. The Act also introduced the 11+ examination, which determined which of three options a child would take at senior school. Those who were proven to be academic enough by the 11+ could go to grammar schools and might end up taking A Levels and going on to university. Others might go to a secondary technical school if they were deemed to be gifted in science and technology, but the vast majority went to a secondary modern, where each school chose its own curriculum.

Up to the age of 11 boys and girls attended primary schools together. The idea of being driven to school was unheard of. Some would cycle but most pupils walked, often in groups with other children from their street but nearly always unaccompanied by their mothers.

School Days

Left *Uniform in every sense of the word, these twins wear the classic Forties school uniform of flannel shorts, knee-length socks, shirt, tie, blazer and cap. Not all schools had caps, but those that did insisted they be worn at all times, otherwise severe punishments would be incurred.*

Right *Looking slightly petrified, a young pupil obediently stands in front of his classmates, reciting* amo, amas, amat *or perhaps his seven times table, while wearing a kilt. If he got it right he might return to his chair with nothing more than a clip round the ear for his trouble.*

The waiting game

The Forties may have been the heyday of Benjamin Britten, but for children in school early music lessons focused on the time-honoured standards, with the emphasis on learning rhythm and timing. Very basic drums were handed out to the children deemed responsible enough not to whack them as hard as they could in whatever time signature took their fancy. For those still grasping the basics of rhythm and behaviour, the triangle was the instrument of choice.

Playing the triangle was something of a double-edged sword. You might find yourself sidelined for most of the piece, while the children with drums or wood blocks made their cacophony of noise, but then your moment would come and if you didn't ding in precisely the right place, everyone would turn and glare at you. Therefore, the triangle required a tremendous capacity for concentration, which alas often proved too much to ask of those upon whom that weighty responsibility was bestowed.

These children are obviously an elite corps of young musicians, all with their eyes on the conductor, except, of course, the trianglists, whose sole focus is on their instrument.

Howzat?!!

A group of boys play cricket in the alley between industrial buildings. It's hardly Lords or The Oval, but for boys with vivid imaginations, that sort of detail was irrelevant. If football was the ultimate street game for boys growing up in the Forties, cricket came a close second. All you needed was a ball and a bat; the stumps could be made up of anything, even three chalk lines drawn on a wall. With players like Don Bradman, Denis Compton and Len Hutton all writing their own chapter in history on the Test pitches of England and Australia at that time, there was no shortage of inspiration for these lads.

The makeshift pitches meant certain unorthodox rules had to be enforced. 'Six and out' was a common one for boys with a tendency to slog the ball over the nearest wall or fence, or in this instance, 'one hand one bounce' for a catch off the wall might apply. Whatever the circumstances, the old mantras of bowling line and length and getting your foot to the pitch of the ball still applied.

Child's play

Playtime at St Peter's London Docks School in Wapping, east London. In the background you can see the masts and funnels of ships in the docks, giving a good indication as to the whereabouts of this school, but for the children it could have been anywhere. The school playground was a place where normal life stopped and imagination took over. For children who had been sitting still in their classrooms all morning, the first inclination was to run around as much as possible. Games like tag, kiss chase and bulldog provided the vague structure for what appeared to the casual onlooker as enthusiastic mayhem. Occasionally two children would bash heads, someone would trip over and graze their knee or a boy might get his head stuck in the school railings, but generally playtime passed off without major injury. A couple of teachers would be on hand just in case anything did go awry and when the time came to return to class they would bring the whole scene to a sudden halt with the simple ringing of a bell.

On me 'ead

A class of boys from a secondary school in Sussex enjoy a chance to get out in the sunshine and play ball. If you look closely you can spot the ball in the middle of the group, within reach of about three of the boys. That, however, doesn't stop the rest of the boys making a play for it like bees round a honeypot, even the one on the far left who must be a good ten feet away.

You will also notice that the boys are wearing nothing but regulation shorts and unbranded black plimsolls with paper-thin soles, highlighting the difference in attitudes between then and now. The simplicity of life back then! No one ever complained. Single sex schools were the norm once children entered senior education and there was no suggestion that boys being made to take their top off for games whatever the weather was anything but healthy, though some PE teachers did enforce it purely to punish or humiliate certain pupils.

A teacher reads to her class as they sit on a fallen tree at a school in Stevenage, Hertfordshire. When the sun shone, the chance to get out of the classroom and 'work' outdoors was always jumped at by pupils and teachers alike.

Two boys and two girls take each other on in the draughts club at an elementary school in Lancashire. Draughts and chess were popular in the Forties, when board games provided a welcome distraction if the weather prevented play outdoors. They were joined later in the decade by Cluedo and Scrabble.

A studious-looking girl gets the full attention of her dormitory mates as she tells them a bedtime story. Boarding schools were very much for the privileged elite and it was not uncommon for a child of the upper classes to be sent away at the age of seven.

*A bunch of schoolboys, still wearing their caps and blazers,
shin up on to a perimeter fence at The Oval in London
to grab a free view of a cricket match. Many boys' first
experience of major sporting events came in this way.
Notice they've brought their own bat, just in case.*

Latchkey kids

During the war years, with fathers away fighting and mothers called up into the workplace, many children found that there was no-one at home at the end of the school day. The term 'latchkey children' was coined for those kids, some of them as young as five years old, who were left to their own devices once school was finished. The expression refers to the fact that they carried their own door key, often on a string around their neck, but for a lot of latchkey children the natural instinct was not to let themselves in and content themselves at home alone, but to meet up with their friends and seek adventure wherever they could. The bombsites and wastelands left by the Blitz became popular stamping grounds for young children, who developed a keen sense of independence, if not daredevil behaviour.

These three lads are killing time watching the ships go by in the Pool of London, using the bombed-out remnants of a warehouse building as their HQ.

The people of Forties Britain may have taken a stoical approach to the austerity that was forced upon them by the war and the period of rebuilding that followed it, but they relished any opportunity to escape from the oppressive environment of the city. The seaside, the countryside, the cinema and the circus were all popular escapes and public holidays would see trains and buses packed with people heading off for a breath of fresh air.

Out and About

In summer the factories would close for two weeks and those workers who had saved up enough money would take a fortnight's holiday in one of the popular seaside resorts. Very few people travelled abroad for their holidays and most relied on public transport to take them away.

Sport also played an important part in keeping the people entertained. Football attracted tens of thousands of spectators every week as the League programme resumed after the war, and the Olympic Games in London in 1948 drew large and enthusiastic crowds, as well as giving people a welcome opportunity to sit in the sun and watch someone else do the work for a change.

People carrier

A man sits aboard his motorbike, about to ride off on a road trip with his wife and six children in the sidecar. As a precaution, he has chosen to wear a flat cap. The girls have ribbons in their hair, but aside from that nobody appears to have considered the possibility of dad losing control and turning the thing over.

Road safety was an embryonic issue in the Forties, probably due to the fact that private vehicle ownership was still rare and petrol rationing limited their use. Approximately one in 20 people owned a car, yet that was enough to present a growing danger. A road safety film from the time states that at least four children every day were being killed in road accidents and 80 injured.

Nevertheless, private vehicles provided a sense of freedom that was hard to resist. The convenience of squeezing your kids into a sidecar, jumping into the saddle and roaring off into the wild blue yonder was a great draw for those lucky enough to be able to afford it.

A group of boys sit on a bridge in Winslow, Buckinghamshire, watching their friends launch a toy boat on the stream. It's a scene of innocence and beauty reminiscent of Enid Blyton's Famous Five books, which became essential reading for young adventurers in the Forties.

Before this method was used for rehabilitating injured horses, children were taught to swim by hooking them with a noose and trawling them through the water. Swimming baths were usually dingy old buildings that had been built in the Victorian era and looked like the water had not been changed since.

Anyone seen baby?

In the Forties, coal was the main energy fuel and the coal mining industry was under immense strain trying to keep up with the growing demand. By the summer of 1946 it was clear that coal stocks were dangerously low and if Britain suffered a harsh winter the country would be thrown into crisis. Despite reassurances from the government, that's exactly what happened. In February 1947 the weather deteriorated, with freezing temperatures not only causing a huge demand for fuel but also making it harder to produce and transport. Non-essential industries were forced to close, soon followed by the power stations themselves. Power cuts became a daily occurrence and as Britain froze, two million factory workers were left idle due to the lack of coal. Miners were brought in from Poland and mines stayed open seven days a week to help increase productivity, but it was only when the weather improved that the crisis began to abate. This group of Londoners is returning from Bow gasworks, where, like so many others, they've had to queue to collect coke to burn in their home fires.

RICH PICKINGS *The end of summer meant free food in the shape of blackberries. Great armies of mothers armed with woodchip punnets would advance on their chosen bramble patch and pick for all they were worth in a co-ordinated attack, for now they could take them home and bake them into delicious pies and crumbles.*

Picnic in the park

Never mind the temperature, if it was sunny on Sunday, families went on a picnic. Note the thick woolly glove lying on the coat in the foreground! This family are celebrating the first day of spring by donning coats and hats and heading down to the park with the picnic basket. Sheltered by a large tree, dad doles out the pop and puffs contentedly on his pipe, while his wife and daughters bask in the heatless glow of the sun.

Picnics weren't just a case of sunning yourself while sitting on a rug eating scones, they were social occasions with activities thrown in. Often they would revolve around some sort of foraging, such as picking bluebells in spring or blackberries in late summer, or they would become mini sports events, with games like rounders to keep the whole family entertained. At the end of the day, everyone would gather up their belongings and head to the bus stop, where they would join the throng of other daytrippers making their way back into the towns and cities.

A bicycle built for three

Guess who looks happiest as dad, mum and child head off on a bicycle holiday. More to the point, who's suffering most? There's nothing quite like a three-seater bike to get a family working together in harmony.

Cycling had enjoyed a boom in popularity between the wars and although the increase in motorised traffic began to drive bicycles off the road in the Forties, the latter years of the decade saw a marked increase in the membership of cycling clubs. The fact was that for many people, especially young people, a bicycle was the only private transport they could afford and, while the roads were becoming increasingly dangerous, cycling clubs provided the opportunity to get out and ride in a safe, sociable and fun way.

The bikes themselves may have looked very similar to those of today, but they weighed a good deal more, being made of tubular steel sections. The keen cyclist usually wore shorts and a loose fitting T-shirt. There was no Lycra and crash helmets were considered unnecessary.

DON'T FALL! Children in a crowd of spectators gasp at the daredevil on the high wire at the Christmas Circus in Haringey, London. The traditional circus was a very popular form of entertainment in the Forties and children from poor families were often invited to attend Christmas rehearsals for free.

Let the Games begin

The sun beats down on wilting spectators at Wembley Stadium during the 1948 Olympic Games. After a decade of hardship, the Games gave Britain a sense that it was emerging into the light in every sense of the word. Fortunately Wembley Stadium had survived the Blitz intact, for there was no provision to build new facilities for the Games. Athletes were housed at an army camp in Uxbridge and in college dormitories and were required to bring their own food.

Though it was dubbed 'the Austerity Olympics', the 1948 Games proved a watershed for technology, in particular television broadcasting. It gave the BBC the chance to show off its prowess to the world and it did so, introducing new cameras and outside broadcast facilities that provided television pictures of a quality never seen before. It was the first time the Games had been held since the war and it proved a fillip for a city – and indeed a world – still recovering from the ravages of the conflict. Fifty-nine countries took part, with Germany and Japan still excluded.

Crowd surfing

When Saturday came, half the country went to the match – the male half. League football was suspended from 1940 to 1946 due to the war, but when it returned it proved a welcome release for men who had spent the week cooped up in factories and offices. At 3 o'clock on Saturday afternoon they would stand packed together on huge sloping terraces to watch the likes of Billy Wright, Tom Finney and Stanley Matthews weave their magic on the pitch. Crowds of 40,000 were commonplace, often rising to 60,000-plus at the bigger grounds. For young boys who accompanied their dads to the game, gaining a view of the pitch was the primary concern. Some would take tea chests to stand on, others would be passed over the heads of the crowd to a place at the front.

Liverpool, Arsenal and Portsmouth were the champions in the three League seasons of the Forties, but the rising star was Manchester United, under new manager Matt Busby, who finished second in each season and won the FA Cup in 1948.

Children perch on a farmer's fence above a flooded field, relishing the chaos of this newly submerged world. By the end of the war black Wellington boots were popular. Thick socks stopped them flopping around your ankles and kids loved to wade in water that nearly came over the top.

Two girls ride a swingboat at a fair on Hampstead Heath. Swingboats were a common attraction at funfairs, giving older children the chance to experience that oscillating feeling they'd enjoyed on the swings as toddlers. It took some effort to get them going, but once you'd got your momentum up, woe betide anyone who got in the way.

CAUTION CHILDREN PLAY HERE

BATTLE FOR THE STREETS

The boys chase a ball, the girls huddle together on the kerb and a truck sits stationary in the background. The street still belonged to the kids, just, but the tide was beginning to turn. Soon the signs would be warning the children to be cautious of traffic, not the other way round.

Riding on a donkey

A group of children on holiday in Blackpool enjoy a
traditional donkey ride on the beach. For people from
the North West, Blackpool had been the major seaside
resort for a hundred years, ever since the railway arrived
there in 1846 and it continued to attract visitors during
the war, despite the threat of German bombing raids on
Britain's coastal towns. In fact, Hitler is believed to have
had his eye on Blackpool as a pleasure resort, had he
succeeded in his plans to conquer Britain. Fortunately, it
was left to the British, who needed no instruction in how
to enjoy the many pleasures of this iconic town. The tower,
the promenade, the beach and the illuminations were all
famous attractions already and the donkey rides on the
beach had been a familiar feature since Victorian times,
when Blackpool had enjoyed its initial boom in popularity.
For most children, this would be their first (and only)
experience of equestrianism and as soon as it was over they
would be pleading for another go.

FEED THE BIRDS *Toddlers give bread and birdseed to the pigeons in Trafalgar Square as their parents keep a watchful eye. Trafalgar Square, which celebrated its centenary in 1944, was renowned for its pigeon population, estimated to number 35,000 at its peak, and feeding them was a highlight for any child on a day trip to the capital.*

Left *Four boys enjoy an impromptu game of football. Footballers in the Forties were hampered somewhat by their attire – thick cotton shirts and shorts and big leather boots – and by the ball itself, which was made of heavy leather and held in shape by a lace, which frequently left its imprint on players' faces.*

Right *A boy stands triumphantly atop a large snowball, wrapped up in coat and beret but with his hands, face and knees exposed. Snow was a regular feature of the Forties, with particularly harsh winters in 1940 and 1947, but for the children it was another welcome distraction from school.*

Certain words will always recur when encapsulating the way of life for Britons in the Forties: austerity, pride, resilience, resourcefulness, spirit. In truth, the Great Depression of the 1930s had prepared people for a life devoid of luxuries and taught them how to make the most of what they had. Added to which, many modern conveniences were yet to be invented or were still in their infancy, so life had an uncomplicated look to it. The custom of scrubbing your front doorstep typified the British trait of keeping up appearances: no matter how hard life might be indoors, you presented a clean, cared-for face to the world.

The Way We Were

But the Forties was also a time of rebuilding, innovation and hope. For many people the war had opened their eyes to new places and new experiences, instilling a greater sense of adventure, a desire to travel and to make the most of life. Coming out of the war, every day brought a growing promise of freedom and prosperity. Food became more plentiful and new conveniences made the work of keeping house much easier.

Home sweet home

A family inspects one of the thousands of prefab houses that were constructed after the war in order to accommodate the people who had been left homeless by the Blitz, which had destroyed nearly half a million homes, and to help with the programme of slum clearance which had begun before the war. Prefabricated housing had been in existence for a hundred years but never had the need been so great. Not only did these buildings provide a fast and cost-effective solution to the housing shortage, they also provided their new occupiers with a standard of living that in many cases was much higher than they were used to. An indoor toilet and a bathroom were standard features – not something that many Britons had experienced at that time. The typical prefab had two bedrooms, a living room and a kitchen and would come with its own small garden plot. Compared to the slums where people lived several to a room, shared toilet facilities with other families in flats above and below, and walked straight out on to the street, this new living environment was pure luxury.

Above *The nuclear family – or should that be the post-nuclear family? – Forties style. Mum does the knitting, dad entertains the little one and son practises his handwriting while taking a break from playing trains. Perhaps the radio is playing. Without television, this is how a typical family might spend the evening together.*

Right *A wire-haired terrier leaps in the air to avoid being sucked up by the vacuum cleaner. Domestic appliances like these started to become much more widely owned among the middle classes after the war, which in turn made the fitting of wall-to-wall carpets more popular.*

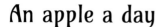

An apple a day

A boy helps himself to one of a plentiful supply of apples as he sits aboard a truck laden with the fruit at harvest time. The war stimulated a boom in the domestic apple market. In response to the call to increase food production, many farmers turned over land previously used for low-yield purposes such as game farming to fruit production, and apples in particular. By the end of the decade the number of apple-growers ran into the thousands, and that didn't count all the households that had planted their own fruit trees in response to the Dig for Victory campaign.

The Cox's Orange Pippin became the number one dessert apple, taking over from the Worcester Pearmain, which had reigned supreme before the war. For children starved of sweets and sugar, apples were a popular source of sweetness and contributed to the general improvement in health. Scrumping – pinching apples from other people's trees – was a common pastime and, though it might result in a clip round the ear, the rewards were worth it.

Errand boy

Kitted out in full livery, a messenger boy sets out to deliver a message to a showgirl from a gentleman in a top hat and moustache. For anyone wanting a message or a gift sent in double-quick time, messenger and telegram services were the way to go and they often employed children barely into their teens. At the start of the decade the school leaving age was 14, which meant a high proportion of children of that age going out into the workplace, usually looking for apprenticeships. The Education Act of 1944 raised the leaving age to 15, a move that caused some concern about a shortfall in the labour force.

Most communication relied on the Royal Mail, although more and more households were being fitted with their own telephone – a classic Bakelite unit with a separate handset and a twist dial on the front. Making phone calls, however, was an expensive luxury and so tight controls were maintained within the home. Often lines would be shared with neighbours, leading to frequent listening in on other people's conversations.

CABBAGE KING *Three boys of ascending sizes labour under the weight of their prize produce as they deliver it to a pub in Kingston-upon-Thames. This would have been a typical errand for boys in the Forties, taking the produce grown in their parents' gardens to wherever it was needed most.*

Two young boys from Essex and Newcastle rock-pooling on the beach at Eastbourne. As people began to travel more after the war, holidays to the seaside provided an opportunity to meet and make friends with children from other parts of the country and then to become penpals, sometimes for life.

*On a bench in Southend, a group of holidaymakers enjoy an ice cream
in the warm summer sun. It was typical for the whole family, parents,
children and grandparents, to take its summer holiday together, especially
as they were often living in the same house.*

Bathing beauties

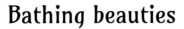

A deckchair attendant takes the time to get to know his customers as they enjoy the sunny weather on Eastbourne beach. The role of women in society changed dramatically during the Forties. Having been conscripted into work during the war, many women were reluctant to return to 'housewife' duties in peacetime and the movement for equal rights gathered momentum. Having begun with a reduction of the pensionable age for women from 65 to 60, the decade saw women promoted to significant leadership roles in politics, the diplomatic service, the Trades Unions and elsewhere. The marriage bar was lifted on women teachers, Post Office workers and Civil Servants and in 1946 a Royal Commission recommended equal pay for women teachers. This newfound power was expressed in the clothes women wore. The practical home-made fashions of the war years gradually gave way to more flamboyant styles, inspired by Christian Dior's New Look of 1947. The previous year the bikini had been invented, encouraging women like these to expose more flesh to the sun, and indeed to the smiling deckchair attendant.

SUN SCREEN *Binoculars, teapots and knotted handkerchiefs are the order of the day for racegoers enjoying Glorious Goodwood in the hot sun. It was normal for people to carry a cotton handkerchief at all times of year, even in hot weather, just in case an impromptu sunhat was required.*

Clowning around

● ●

The crowd seem more interested in the camera than the clown as he goes through his routine at a circus in Bristol. Circuses were still held in permanent buildings a lot of the time, although travelling tented circuses had enjoyed a boom in popularity across Europe between the wars. With radio still the only form of light entertainment in most households, going out to the theatre, cinema and circus was a popular pastime in the Forties. Famous circus names like Chipperfield and Billy Smart were rising to prominence, but the biggest draw of all was Bertram Mills Circus, which put on a Christmas show every year at Olympia and boasted the Royal Family and Winston Churchill among its enthusiastic patrons.

Acts were fast-moving and typically included horseback stunts, gymnastics and trapeze acts and always some high jinks from the clowns. It was also a chance to see a menagerie of exotic animals, often whipped into a fury by their 'tamers'. The 1948 Bertram Mills summer season tour featured 130 animals, including elephants, bears, lions and monkeys.

Pile 'em high

A typical grocer's shop in London's Blackfriars. The hurricane lamps are not so typical – they became necessary during the power cuts of 1947 when the country's coal supplies ran low and the harsh winter created an unsustainable demand. The scales are typical, as are the shelves stacked with jars and tins of preserves and chopped fruits and pulses. The boxes of cereals don't offer a vast choice, but some of these were staples that would stand the test of time.

This was the way people did their food shopping in the Forties. The idea of self-service was only just beginning to catch on and instead you would queue at the counter and the shop assistant would fetch down all your grocery needs. Rationing meant that shopping lists were always kept small and diets depended more on what you could grow at home or buy fresh from the butcher's and greengrocer's. But Birds Eye had introduced frozen food just before the war and in 1950 Sainsbury's would open its first self-service store in Croydon. The age of the traditional grocer's shop was slowly coming to an end.

Two unshakeable British traditions held true during the Forties in spite of the upheaval, the austerity and the loss: namely queuing and rain. These people are managing to combine the two as they wait at Waterloo Station to board a train for their summer holidays.

A typical British gent studying the racing form on his way to Epsom for the Derby. He could just as well be on the train to work in the City, the suit and tie, bowler hat and newspaper being the standard dress for anyone working in the banking business of the Forties.

Filling station

• •

Children from a school in Kent line up to have their teeth examined in a mobile dentist and clinic. The Forties brought a radical reform in healthcare with the introduction of the National Health Service in 1948. For the first time, all aspects of the medical services were brought together under one umbrella and made available to all for free. Under the previous system, only those who paid national insurance (mostly men) were covered for medical treatment. Everyone else had to pay and consequently many chose, or were forced, to forgo treatment altogether.

The public response was enthusiastic, with 97 per cent of people registering with GPs. Indeed, the take-up in NHS services proved much heavier than had been forecast and the system of funding the service through taxation immediately came under strain. For children, the dread of the dentist's drill and the sight – albeit blurred – of the optician's test chart became familiar features of a life in which good health came to be regarded as a basic human right.

Bobbies on the beat

Five police constables take notes during their briefing
before going out on the night beat. The image of the British
'bobby' conjures up a time when everybody respected the
police and children who found themselves on the wrong
side of a dressing-down from the local constable would feel
the sting for a long time. Yet the truth is that the Forties
was far from an idyllic time for the forces of law and order.
The war brought a rapid rise in crime, as opportunists
took to looting and selling rationed goods on the black
market, and the trend continued after the war. Austerity
and the traumatic effects of the conflict drove people to
crime in unprecedented numbers. By the end of the decade
the crime rate had risen tenfold from the levels of 20
years before. To combat this, the police had to make do
with limited equipment. They had been armed during the
war so that they could be ready in case of invasion, but in
peacetime their equipment amounted to little more than
a truncheon, a torch and a whistle.

WRITING ON THE WALL *Two boys with stray dogs amid the graffiti-covered walls of the Gorbals area of Glasgow. The graffiti appears to have been drawn by somebody practising for a geometry exam, or perhaps it was a statement that these walls were like a cage.*

Warm welcome

A West Indian immigrant, just off the boat in Liverpool, walks the streets with his suitcase, looking for accommodation. The Forties saw the start of a wave of immigration from the Commonwealth and in those early days there was a general sense of welcome. These were men who had enlisted and fought for the Allies during the war and were now helping to fill a sizeable hole in the labour market. The influx began with the arrival of the SS *Empire Windrush* at Tilbury in June 1948, carrying around 500 Jamaican men. In the interests of the war effort and the subsequent rebuilding, UK law had effectively conferred citizenship on anyone from the Commonwealth, thus paving the way for more to follow and take their place in the workforce.

They were augmented by a large Polish contingent, many of whom had come to Britain in the wake of the German invasion and now found their country under Soviet rule. They too were welcomed with open arms and the British people began to get a first-hand perspective of the world that they had been fighting for.

SEEING THE SIGHTS *A group of Manchester United fans take a detour past Buckingham Palace on their way to Wembley for the 1948 FA Cup Final. The oldest cup competition in football was the high point of the season and those without a ticket would gather round the nearest radio to listen to the match.*

Two euphonium players perform as part of a brass band in the Pennines. Traditional brass bands were still very active in the Forties, particularly in the north of England where they were formed of colliery and factory workers, but the genre was beginning to wane in the face of new, more exotic forms of music arriving from elsewhere.

A pair of Pearlies in full regalia. The London tradition of Pearly Kings and Queens only started in the late 19th century but by the Forties it was in full swing, with one Pearly family for each London borough, all helping to raise money for needy causes.

And the winner is...

Six beauties squeeze on to the podium at Butlin's holiday camp hoping to win the title of Butlin's Girl of the Week. The Forties saw Butlin's cement its place in the hearts of British holidaymakers. Having opened his first two camps in Skegness and Clacton in the 1930s, Billy Butlin was forced to postpone operations during the war and handed his camps over for use as military bases. But when the war ended, Skegness and Clacton reopened to the public and were joined by new camps in Filey, Ayr and Pwllheli. Every February, winners of Butlin's beauty contests would appear at a Festival of Reunion at the Royal Albert Hall. This pageant helped to prepare the ground for the Miss World contest, which was launched in 1951. At a time when women were establishing equal rights and able to become graduates of Cambridge University for the first time (1948), the sight of girls parading in swimsuits and bikinis was not without controversy. But these were early days for women's liberation and it was the liberation of women from the dowdy fashions of wartime that carried the day.

Left *Crowds dancing at a Farewell Ball at Butlin's. Having spent the week making the most of a range of activities and entertainments, all for the price of an average week's wages, Butlin's clientele let their hair down in one final show of abandonment before returning to their factories and offices.*

Above *Two members of the Women's Auxiliary Air Force (WAAF) get into costume for a 1940 pantomime production in aid of the Spitfire Fund. The Forties was a heyday for pantomime and comedy in general, as stars like Max Miller and Arthur Askey helped distract the public from the daily grind.*

Full steam ahead

Men at the Crewe railway works apply the finishing touches to a sleek new locomotive. The Forties was still the age of steam – perhaps its last Golden Age. The train was the predominant mode of transport for people who wished to travel long distances and engine designers had refined the steam locomotive into a beautiful streamlined powerhouse that could achieve speeds well in excess of 100mph. A year before war broke out, *Mallard*, a class A4 locomotive built by the London and North Eastern Railway company (LNER), set a world speed record for a steam train of 125.88 mph. The record would never be broken.

The railways were mostly run by four big operators, LNER, the Great Western Railway (GWR), the London, Midland and Scottish Railway (LMS) and the Southern Railway (SR). In 1948 the network was nationalized, becoming British Railways. Smaller branch lines, deemed unsustainable, were closed and the face of the British railway network began to change forever.

The sun sets on the Isle of Wight as a man and his children take one last donkey ride. The Forties were drawing to a close, the war was fading into history and the country was ready to welcome in a new age of hope, prosperity and progress.